Strategic Statistics

Stephanie Loureiro

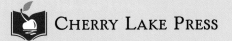

Published in the United States of America by Cherry Lake Publishing Group
Ann Arbor, Michigan
www.cherrylakepublishing.com

Reading Adviser: Beth Walker Gambro, MS, Ed., Reading Consultant, Yorkville, IL

Photo Credits: Cover: ©OnstOn / Getty Images; ©Natalia Darmoroz / Getty Images; ©Aryo Hadi / Getty Images; ©ginosphotos / Getty Images; ©Shendart / Getty Images; page 5: ©Jessica Orozco; page 10: ©Jessica Orozco; page 16: ©Net Vector / Shutterstock; page 19: ©Designer / Getty Images; page 19: ©ozcan yalaz / Getty Images; page 20: ©ColourCreatype / Shutterstock; page 20: ©matsabe / Shutterstock; page 24: ©Jessica Orozco; page 25: ©Jessica Orozco; page 26: ©Eric Broder Van Dyke / Shutterstock; page 28: ©JoeSAPhotos / Shutterstock; page 30: ©Nikolai V Titov / Shutterstock

Cherry Lake Press is an imprint of Cherry Lake Publishing Group.

Library of Congress Cataloging-in-Publication Data
Library of Congress Cataloging-in-Publication Data has been filed and is available at catalog.loc.gov.

Cherry Lake Publishing Group would like to acknowledge the work of the Partnership for 21st Century Learning, a Network of Battelle for Kids. Please visit *http://www.battelleforkids.org/networks/p21* for more information.

Printed in the United States of America

Note from publisher: Websites change regularly, and their future contents are outside of our control. Supervise children when conducting any recommended online searches for extended learning opportunities.

Stephanie Loureiro is a writer and editor. She's been writing since she was nine years old and loves working on books that help kids discover things they love. When she's not writing, she can be found curled up reading a book, doing Olympic weightlifting, or singing loudly and dancing around to Taylor Swift. She currently lives in Idaho with her husband, daughter, and two dogs.

CONTENTS

Stats and Sports

Modern sports have been popular in the United States for a long time. They got more popular over the past 100 years. They really took off after the 1950s. People soon started to keep track of their favorite teams. They kept track of their favorite players, too. They wanted to know how well they were doing. That's where statistics and analytics came in.

Statistics is a science. It is for studying data. Analytics is the information learned from that. Both are used for rankings. They can find top players and teams. They guess winners. They also evaluate roster picks and more!

Average Game Attendance

MAJOR LEAGUE
BASEBALL (MLB)
26,483 people

NATIONAL BASKETBALL
ASSOCIATION (NBA)
17,184 people

NATIONAL FOOTBALL
LEAGUE (NFL)
69,615 people

NATIONAL HOCKEY
LEAGUE (NHL)
15,841 people

2019, Forbes; 2022 Statista; 2022 Sports Business Journal

## CHAPTER 1

All About the Numbers

Most major sports use analytics. There is one sport that uses it the most. It is baseball! It was the first to use analytics. People use stats to make predictions. They guess how players will do. This gives teams a winning edge. Batting average is an example. It tells you how well a player might do when they are at bat. It is found like this:

player's total # of hits / player's total # of at bats

Imagine you are watching a baseball game. There are runners on each base. There are two outs. This means the hitting team has one chance to score. The coach will know to use a good hitter. The coach will send in a player with a high batting average. This gives the team better odds at bringing the runs in.

BASEBALL TERMS:

hits: when a batter hits the ball with the bat and the ball does not go past foul lines

Average Baseball Stats

Batting Average
(player's hits / player's total at bats)

Home Runs
(total number of home runs
a player hits)

BA:
.330

HR:
44

RBIs:
139

Runs Batted In
(total number of runs a player
scored because of their at bats)

**The player who leads the league in
these three wins the Triple Crown.
And the Triple Crown goes to . . .
Miguel Cabrera of the Detroit Tigers!**

2022, Baseball-Reference.com

History of Sports Analytics

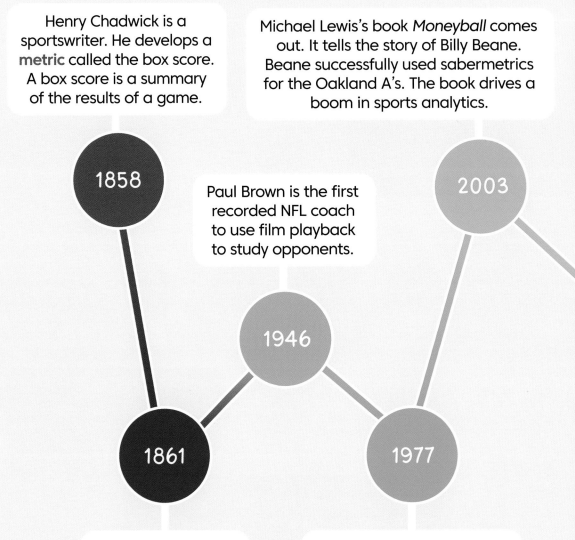

Henry Chadwick is a sportswriter. He develops a **metric** called the box score. A box score is a summary of the results of a game.

Michael Lewis's book *Moneyball* comes out. It tells the story of Billy Beane. Beane successfully used sabermetrics for the Oakland A's. The book drives a boom in sports analytics.

1858

Paul Brown is the first recorded NFL coach to use film playback to study opponents.

2003

1946

1861

1977

The first written sports analysis is made. It's a book called *Beadle's Dime Base-Ball Player*.

Bill James comes up with a mathematical system. Called sabermetrics, it evaluates baseball players.

The Philadelphia Eagles rely heavily on analytics during the 2017–2018 season. They go on to win the Super Bowl.

Still driven by analytics, the Eagles returned to the Super Bowl in 2023.

The NFL hires a full-time data analyst.

2017 - 2023

2007

2004

2013

Dean Oliver writes *Basketball on Paper*. This becomes a must-have handbook for basketball analysis.

The NBA becomes the first American sports league to use **player tracking** in every game.

Common Stats of Major Sports

- All pro sports use stats. They track player and team performance in some way.

- Some stats are simple counts. They can last for a season or a player's career. Or they can last for the entire league history.

- Other stats use equations.

NHL

Shooting Percentage:
# of goals made / # of shots taken

Saving Percentage:
# of saves / total # of shots on goal

Goals Against Average:
(# of goals against x 60) / # of minutes played

Time on Ice:
total number of minutes a player is on the ice during a game

NFL

Point Differential:
# of points a team scores — # of points a team allows

Success Rate (SR; for running backs):
# of successful plays / total plays

Field Goal Percentage (FG%):
# of made shots / total # of shot attempts

NBA

Free Throw Percentage (FT%):
# of free throws made / total # of attempts

Effective Field Goal Percentage (EFG%):
[(# of field goals made + 0.5) x # of 3-point field goals made] /
# of field goals attempted

3-Point Field Goal Percentage (3P%):
# of 3-points made / # 3-point attempts

MLB

Batting Average (BA):
# of hits a player / # of at bats

On-Base Percentage (OB%):
(hits + walks + hit-by-pitches) /
(at bats + walks + hit-by-pitches + sacrifice flies)

Earned Run Average (ERA):
9 x (earned runs / innings pitched)

BASEBALL TERMS:

at bats: times when a batter gets on base because a fielder is making a play at another base

earned runs: runs that are scored because of a pitch instead of a fielding error

hit-by-pitches: times when a batter is hit by a ball without swinging at it

on-base percentage: how often a batter gets on base

sacrifice flies: times when a batter hits a fly ball to the outfield or into foul territory to allow a runner to score

walks: times when a pitcher throws four pitches out of the strike zone, but the hitter does not swing at any of them.

## CHAPTER 2

Moneymaking Stats

Stats can be used to predict how games turn out. Some people make money this way. They do it by betting. College basketball is a popular sport for this. March Madness is a college basketball tournament. It takes place in the United States. It happens every spring. People guess which teams will make it to the playoffs. They also guess who will win the championship.

But sports stats can be used for other things, too. They can decide the winners of awards or how much players get paid. Statistics can even change the price of tickets and how many tickets are sold.

March Madness: Percent Chance of Reaching the Final Four

Teams are referred to as "seeds." The team with the best record is the number one seed. The team with the second-best record is the number two seed and so on. The number is assigned by the team's season record or win percentage (games won / total games played).

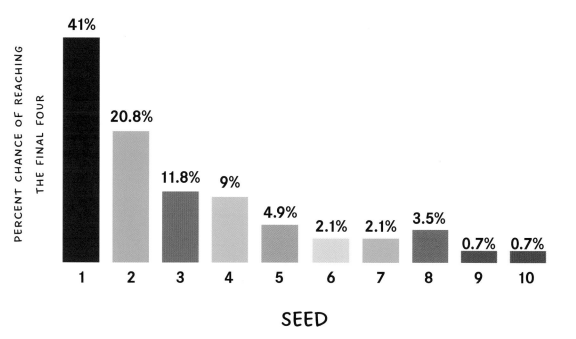

2022, BoydBets.com

Top 12 2022 NFL Total Team Salaries

Fans betting on teams isn't the only way people make money with stats. Teams and players can, too. The NFL has an annual spending cap for how much a team can pay its players in total, called salaries. The cap is decided by how much revenue the NFL made in the last season. There are three types of revenue that matter. They are league media revenue, NFL ventures and postseason revenue, and local revenue. Ticket sales are part of revenue. It is important for players and teams to perform well. Sales go down if they don't. Fewer ticket sales means less total money. And that means a smaller salary. Revenue and salary are very important. There is a whole world of stats analysis devoted to them.

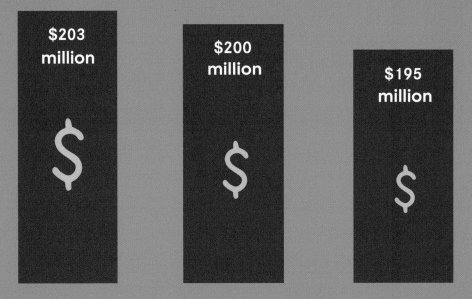

$203 million — Los Angeles Chargers

$200 million — Jacksonville Jaguars

$195 million — Cincinnati Bengals

New York Jets	$195 million
Indianapolis Colts	$192 million
Kansas City Chiefs	$191 million
Miami Dolphins	$191 million
New England Patriots	$190 million
Washington Commanders	$188 million
Tennessee Titans	$185 million
San Francisco 49ers	$185 million
Baltimore Ravens	$184 million

2022, Over the Cap

Fan attendance is another stat that is calculated and tracked carefully. Fans play a role in how much money a team makes. If a team is not playing well, the number of fans going to games goes down. When a team does well, more fans go to games. When more fans go to games, the team makes more money.

FAST FACTS

- Most pro teams use dynamic pricing. This means prices can change because of real-world factors. One of these is how many people want to buy tickets. Another is if the results of the game are important for the championships.

- Ticket sales can be influenced by how "good" of a game it might be. Good games can be the top two teams in the league. Or it could be two teams that are rivals.

- If a team is in a playoff or championship game, ticket prices tend to go up. Final games or championships cost more. For example, the average price of a ticket to the 2022 Super Bowl was $10,000.

Houston Astros Fan Attendance

In 2015, the Houston Astros started to play better than they had before. They won more games. They made it to championship games. Fans bought more tickets because of this. The team uses these stats to predict future sales.

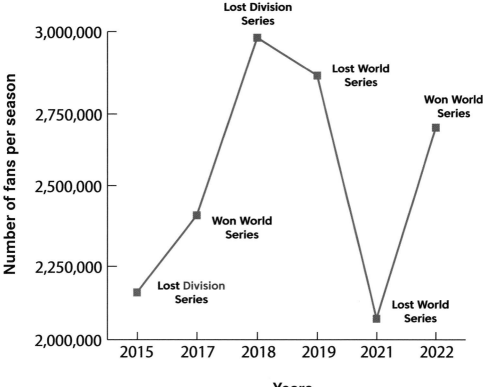

BASEBALL TERMS:

division: how the 30 teams in the MLB are grouped to play each other

2022, Baseball-Reference.com

## CHAPTER 3

The Future of Sports Stats

Some people really like sports statistics and analytics. So they do it for a living! Sports analytics is now a global industry. It might be worth up to $22 billion by 2030. There are many jobs a person could have. They could be sports statisticians or data analysts. They could be talent scouts. Talent scouts go to high school and college games to find good players. There are skills needed for these jobs. Some of the skills are math, research, and data analysis. People who want to have these careers study math or statistics in college.

College Majors of Sports Statisticians

Skills Needed for Sports Statisticians

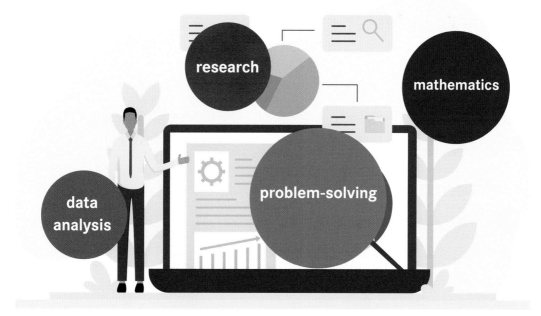

Worldwide Growth of Sports Analytics

Growth Rates

High

Medium

Low

No Info

Drivers of Growth

 American football  Cricket

 Baseball Hockey

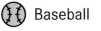 Basketball Soccer

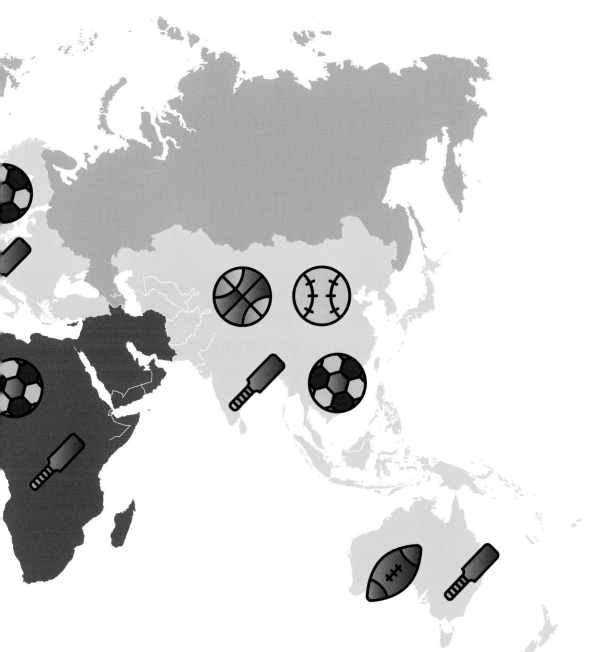

2022, Mordor Intelligence

## CHAPTER 4

Record-Breaking Stats

Breaking a record is a big deal. There are many kinds of records. It can be hard to keep track. Statistics is a way to keep track. It can track records in league and team histories. Some records are held for many years before they are broken. But why does it take so long to break them? Some records are statistically harder to break. For example, Ty Cobb played in the early 1900s. He still holds the record for highest career batting average, with .3662. It's rare for baseball players to have a batting average over .350. Over .360 is very rare.

NBA Records

90.82%

HIGHEST FREE THROW PERCENTAGE, HELD BY STEPHEN CURRY

Free Throw Percentage: # of free throws made / total # of attempts

30.12

HIGHEST POINTS PER GAME AVERAGE (REGULAR SEASON), HELD BY MICHAEL JORDAN

Points per Game Average: total # of points scored / total # of games played

2022, NBA

45.4%

HIGHEST 3-POINT PERCENTAGE, HELD BY STEVE KERR

3-Point Percentage: # of 3-points made / # 3-point attempts

NHL: They Shoot, They Score

80%

Highest shootout scoring percentage held by Petteri Nummelin

Shootout Scoring Percentage:
# of goals made / # of shots taken

Highest face-off winning percentage held by Yanic Perreault

62.86%

Face-off Win Percentage:
# of face-offs won / # of face-offs taken

HOCKEY TERMS:

shootout: when a game ends in a tie and each team is given the chance to take three shots

face-off: when the referee drops the puck between two players, the first player to get possession of the puck wins the face-off

Wayne Gretzky: The Great One

17.6%

WAYNE GRETZKY'S CAREER SHOOTING PERCENTAGE

Shooting Percentage:
goals made / number of shots taken

41%

Percent by which he broke the previous record

1986

Year he set all-time single-season points record

2022, statmuse.com; 2022, The Atlantic

FAST FACTS

- Each baseball game has 12,386,344 possible plays.
- A baseball game usually lasts 3 hours. It only has about 10 minutes of actual play time. That's only 5.5%!
- Ted Williams has the highest career on-base percentage in MLB history. It is .4816.
- The highest batting average in baseball history is held by Ty Cobb. It is .366212.

MLB Records

.864%
highest stolen base percentage (SB%) – Carlos Beltrán

Stolen Base Percentage:
# of steals / # of attempts

.6094%
highest single-season on-base percentage (OBP) – Barry Bonds

.426%
highest single-season batting average (BA) – Nap Lajoie

.9847%
highest career in-field fielding percentage (FP) – Omar Vizquel

1.82
lowest earned run average (ERA) – Ed Walsh

Fielding Percentage:
(put outs + assists) / (put outs + assists + errors)

FAST FACTS

- Tom Brady holds the record for most regular season wins (251).
- Drew Brees holds the record for quarterback with the most 400-yard games (16).
- The most touchdown passes in a single season is 55. This record is held by Peyton Manning.

Football Records

105.8

Highest passing rating held by Patrick Mahomes
Passing Rating: (# of completions / attempts – .3) x 5

67.8%

Highest completion percentage held by Deshaun Watson
Completion Percentage:
(% of passes thrown for completions – 30) x .05

47.6

Highest yards per punt tied between Michael Dickson
and Shane Lechler
Yards per Punt (sometimes known as punt yardage):
total yards / total # of punts

FOOTBALL TERMS:

completion: when a receiver catches a forward pass thrown by the quarterback without the ball touching the ground

punt: a kick performed by dropping the ball from the hands and then kicking the ball before it hits the ground.

2022, The Atlantic

Activity

Predict the Winner

Want to practice your statistical skills? Put them to the test by creating your own March Madness bracket!

Materials Needed

- Computer access
- Paper
- Writing utensil

1. Research statistics from the previous college basketball season. Look at the team stats and compare them. Be sure to keep the honor system. Don't peek at which teams made it to the finals!

2. Draw a blank bracket. See the example below. Then use your stat research to fill it in and make your predictions.

3. Ask family and friends to make their own brackets. Then research the outcome of March Madness for that season. Compare your bracket to your friends' and families' brackets. Did your stat research help you predict correctly?

GAME 1

Team A

Winner of GAME 1

Team B

GAME 3

Winner of GAME 3

Team C

Winner of GAME 2

Team D

GAME 2

Learn More

Books

Berglund, Bruce R. *Football GOATs: The Greatest Athletes of All Time*. North Mankato, MN: Capstone Press, 2022.

Buckley, James, Jr. *It's a Numbers Game: Baseball.* Washington, DC: National Geographic Kids, 2021.

Swanson, Jennifer. *The Secret Science of Sports: The Math, Physics, and Mechanical Engineering behind Every Grand Slam, Triple Axel, and Penalty Kick*. New York: Black Dog & Leventhal, 2021.

Online Resources to Explore with an Adult

Sports Illustrated Kids

Sports Reference

Bibliography

Abee, Jerrod. "The Slow Growth of Data Analytics in the Football." Samford University. January 6, 2022.

Kashyap, Hitesh. "A Primer on Sports Analytics: A New Dimension of Sports." Analytics India Magazine. August 5, 2021.

Steinberg, Leigh. "Changing the Game: The Rise of Sports Analytics." Forbes. August 18, 2015.

Thompson, Derek. "The Most Amazing Statistical Achievement in U.S. Sports History." The Atlantic. January 21, 2022.

Glossary

analytics (an-uh-LIH-tiks) the careful study of information in order to find patterns and come to conclusions

betting (BET-ing) an activity where you make a guess about an outcome and risk losing something if you are wrong

data (DAY-tuh) numbers and facts about a certain subject that are collected and studied

equations (ee-KWAY-shuns) statements that use mathematics to find answers

evaluate (ee-VAL-yoo-ate) to study in order to determine significance, worth, or condition

industry (IN-duh-stree) a group of businesses that provide a similar service

league (LEEG) an organized group of sports teams that play against each other

media (MEE-dee-uh) the ways info is given to the public, including newspapers, radio, television, and the internet

metric (MEH-trick) a type of measurement

player tracking (PLAY-ur TRAK-ing) technology used to collect information about sports players and their performance

predictions (pruh-DIK-shuns) statements about what might happen in the future

revenue (REH-vuh-noo): money that is made by a business or group

statistics (stuh-TISS-tikz) a branch of math that studies information in order to draw conclusions

ventures (VEN-tuhrs) new activities, projects, or business actions that are somewhat risky

Index